Card Games

Authors

John Belton
Joella Cramblit

RAINTREE EDITIONS

Library of Congress Number:
75-42319
Printed in the United States of America

Published by

 RAINTREE EDITIONS

A Division of Raintree
Publishers Limited
Milwaukee, Wisconsin 53203

Distributed by Childrens Press
1224 West Van Buren Street
Chicago, Illinois 60607

Library of Congress Cataloging in Publication Data

Belton, John, 1931—
   Card games.

   SUMMARY: Step-by-step directions and color illustrations explain the rules and strategy of card games.
   1. Cards—Juvenile literature. [1. Cards. 2. Games] I. Cramblit, Joella, joint author. II. Title.
GV1244.B43   795.4   75-42319
ISBN 0-8172-0022-3
ISBN 0-8172-0021-5 lib. bdg.

1

Concentration

PLAYERS

Two to ten

OBJECT OF THE GAME

To collect more pairs of cards than the other players. A pair of cards is two cards with the same number or rank.

DEALER

Each player picks a card from the deck to decide who will deal. The player with the highest card is the dealer. Ace is high. The deal passes to the left with each new game.

THE DEAL

Shuffle the cards. Spread the deck face down on a large table or on the floor. The cards may be laid out in any pattern, but no two cards should touch each other.

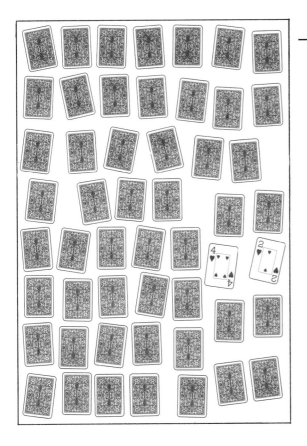

HOW TO PLAY CONCENTRATION

1. When you play Concentration you must try to remember the position of each card on the table or floor.

2. The dealer starts the game by turning face up any two cards, one at a time. All the players look at the two cards as they are turned up. The two cards are not picked up, just turned face up.

3. If the two cards are a pair, the dealer picks them up, keeps them, and turns up two more cards. The dealer's turn continues as long as the two cards turned up are a pair.

4. If the two cards are not a pair, they are turned face down and left in their original places. This ends the dealer's turn.

   Remember: Cards are picked up *only* when they are a pair.

5. After the dealer's turn is over, the player to the left of the dealer continues the game. Play continues around the table to the left.

6. Each player tries to remember which cards are turned up and their exact locations. Remembering where the cards are can help a player win the game. For example, suppose

that a King was turned up, but was not paired with another card. It was turned face down. Now it's your turn, and the card you turn up is a King. If you remember where the first King is, turn it up, and you'll have a pair of cards to pick up.

7. Every time a pair is turned up, the player picks them up, keeps them, and continues to try to match cards.

8. A player's turn ends when two cards that are not pairs are turned up.

9. The winner is the player who is holding the greatest number of pairs after all the cards have been picked up from the pile.

HOW TO SCORE

1. Write down each player's name.

2. Determine the winner by counting the number of pairs each player is holding.

3. Only the winner—the player with the greatest number of pairs—gets a score. Each pair is worth 1 point. All other players get 0 as their score for that game.

4. Play until one person gets 100 points.

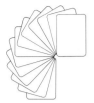

2

Thirty-One *Skip*

PLAYERS

Two to ten

OBJECT OF THE GAME

To get 31 points—or as close to 31 as possible—before any other player

DEALER

Each player picks a card from the deck to decide who will deal. The player with the highest card is the dealer. Ace is high. The deal passes to the left with each new game.

THE DEAL

Deal three cards, one at a time, to each player. The cards not dealt make up the draw pile. Put the draw pile face down in the middle of the table. Turn up the top card of the draw pile to start the discard pile, and put this card face up next to the draw pile.

Draw Pile

Discard Pile

1. The cards that are combined to equal 31 points—or close to 31 points—must all be of the same suit.

2. The point values of the cards are:

   a. Each Ace equals 11 points.

   b. Each King, Queen, Jack, or 10 equals 10 points.

   c. All other cards equal their face value. A Club 2 is worth 2 points, a Club 3 is worth 3 points, and so on.

3. The perfect score is 31. The combinations that equal 31 are:

   a. An Ace and two face cards of the same suit or,

   b. An Ace, a face card, and a 10 of the same suit.

   You won't always be able to combine three cards that equal 31.

4. To begin the game, the player to the left of the dealer picks either the top card from the draw pile or the top card from the discard pile. The player, who is now holding four cards,

looks at them to see if there are three cards of the same suit that together equal 31, or close to 31 points.

5. The player keeps the three best cards, then discards one card face up on top of the discard pile. In this way, no player ever ends a turn holding more than three cards.

6. Play continues around the table to the left. Each player picks and discards, trying to get three cards that equal 31 points (or close to 31). After a player picks from the draw pile or discard pile and has 31 points (or a hand the player thinks will beat everyone else), the player must wait until the next turn before doing or saying anything. On the next turn, instead of picking a card, the player knocks once on the table. This knock lets the other players know that they have one more turn to "improve" their hand.

Important: A player cannot pick a card and knock on the same turn.

7. After a player knocks, the playing continues around the table one more time and ends with the player who knocked.

8. At this point, all players must

show their cards. The player
with the best hand wins.

9. The only time a player does
   not have to knock is when the
   player is dealt three cards that
   equal 31 points. When this
   happens, the player says, "31"
   right away and wins the game.
   If two players are dealt hands
   that equal 31, the first player to
   say "31" wins.

10. Sometimes, two players have
    the same number of points
    when all players show their
    cards. If this happens, the
    player with the highest ranking
    card wins, as in this example:

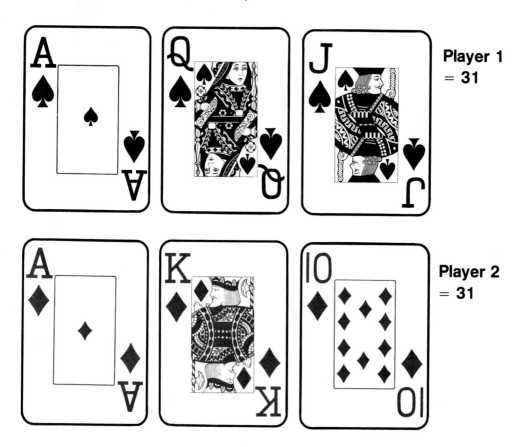

Player 1 = 31

Player 2 = 31

In this game, Player 2 wins because the King ranks higher than the Queen.

Also, a Queen ranks higher than a Jack, and a Jack ranks higher than a 10.

SAMPLE GAME

1. Player 1 (the player to the left of the dealer) is holding a Spade Ace, a Heart 10, and a Club 4.

2. Player 1 can now pick one card from the discard pile or one card from the draw pile.

3. Player 1 picked a Heart Ace and discarded the Club 4. Now Player 1 holds 21 points in Hearts: The Heart Ace is worth 11 points and the Heart 10 is worth 10 points.

4. If Player 1 thought that this hand—totaling 21 points— would beat everyone else's hand, Player 1 could knock on the next turn.

5. Player 2, to the left of Player 1, continues the game by picking a card from the draw pile or the discard pile. Player 2's turn is over when he or she discards a card.

6. Play continues around the table with each player to the left of the last one taking his or her turn.

7. The winner is the player with the most points—either 31 points, or a total closer to 31 than any other player.

STRATEGY

1. Sometimes it is good strategy to knock early in the game with 21 points. It could be that no one else is holding a better hand.

2. It is also good strategy to knock on your first turn instead of picking a card if you are dealt a good hand, for example, 21 points.

HOW TO SCORE

1. Write down each player's name. Only the person with the most points gets a score. Everyone else gets 0 for that game. For example:

   a. Player 1 has 31 points.

   b. All the other players have less than 31.

   c. The score sheet looks like this:

Player 1	Player 2	Player 3	Player 4
31	0	0	0

2. You may want to play until one person has 100 points.

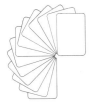

3

Speed

PLAYERS

Two

OBJECT OF THE GAME

To be the first player out of cards

DEALER

Each player picks a card from the deck to decide who will deal. The player with the highest card is the dealer. Ace is low, King is high. After the first deal, take turns dealing.

THE DEAL

There are three parts to the deal: the hand, the reserve pile, and the draw pile.

The hand: Deal five cards to each player one at a time. These are the cards the players hold in their hands.

The reserve pile: Deal two piles of seven cards one at a time. Keep these two piles face down. Put one pile to the right and one pile to the left of the center of the table.

The draw pile: Deal the remaining

cards one at a time to make two
draw piles. Put one pile face down
in front of each player near the
center of the table.

The deal looks like this:

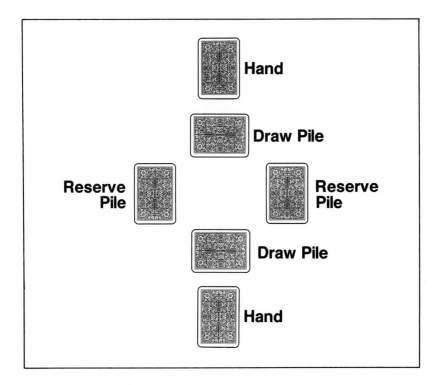

HOW TO PLAY SPEED

1. This is a very exciting game if
   you play your cards quickly.
   You do not take turns playing
   cards. Both players play their
   cards at the same time and try
   to be the first one out of cards.
   The name of the game is
   Speed!

2. Before beginning the game,
   each player at the same time
   turns up the top card from one
   of the two reserve piles. These

two cards form the building piles. Put these two cards face up between the two reserve piles, like this:

Reserve Pile

Building Piles

Reserve Pile

3. Cards are played onto the building piles in the following way:

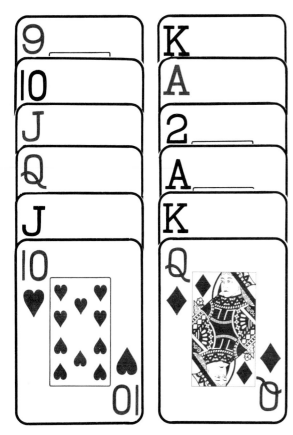

a. You can play a card that is either one number *higher* or one number *lower* than the face-up card. For example: A 2 or a King can play on an Ace.

b. The card does not have to be a certain suit or color. Only numbers are important in this game.

You must play one number lower or one number higher than the top card on either of the building piles. In the illustration, the cards are played in a long column so you can see them. When you play a game, however, play the cards one on top of the other.

15

4. Pick up the five cards that make up your hand. It is not necessary to sort your cards. It is important that you always have five cards in your hand. When you have less than five cards, you must draw a card from the draw pile in front of you.

5. The game begins as soon as both players have turned up the top cards from the two reserve piles to form the building piles.

6. Both players should begin building on *either* one of the building piles immediately, using the cards in their hand. The idea is for each player to play cards quickly, before the other player can.

7. Remember, you must always keep five cards in your hand. When you play a card onto a building pile, you must pick a card from your draw pile to add to your hand.

8. Keep building on either of the building piles and drawing cards as quickly as possible from the draw pile in front of you. The pattern is from the cards in your hand, to the building pile, to the draw pile, and back to your hand.

9. When neither player can play a card on the building piles, then

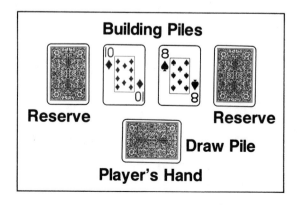

16

both players turn up one card from their reserve pile at the same time. They use the card from the reserve pile to begin playing again on the building piles.

10. Sometimes all the cards from the reserve pile are turned up before the game is over and neither player can make a play. When this happens, each player picks up one building pile, turns it face down, and starts a new reserve pile.

11. The game continues. Each player turns up the top card of one of the new reserve piles to start a building pile. Again, each player begins playing cards onto either building pile.

12. Because you must always have five cards in your hand, no one can win until all of the cards in a player's own draw pile are gone, as well as all of the cards that the player is holding.

13. The winner is the first player out of cards.

HOW TO SCORE

1. Scoring is very easy for Speed. The winner of each game gets 1 point.

2. You may want to play until one player gets 10 points.

4

Ninety-Eight

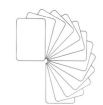

PLAYERS

Two to eight

OBJECT OF THE GAME

To avoid playing a card that will make the total of the cards played equal 98 or more

THE DEALER

Each player picks a card from the deck to decide who will deal. The player with the highest card is the dealer. Ace is low, King is high. The deal passes to the left with each new game.

THE DEAL

Shuffle the cards. Deal three cards face down one at a time to each player from left to right. Put the rest of the deck face down in the middle of the table. This is the draw pile.

HOW TO PLAY NINETY-EIGHT

1. In this game you add the point values of the cards together as each player plays a card.

2. The player who plays a card to

equal 98 or more loses and the game ends.

3. Suits are *not* important in this game, only numbers.

4. The point value of the cards are:

   a. Ace equals 1.

   b. The 2 through 9 equal their face value.

   c. Jack and King equal 10 points.

   d. The 10 equals minus 10 (10 points off). When you play a 10, subtract 10 points from the total of the cards already played, as in this example: A 5 and a 9 have been played, equaling 14 (5+9). A 10 is played next. Now the total is 4 (14−10).

   e. The Queen equals 0. When you play a Queen, the total of the cards played stays the same: A 5 and a 9 have been played, equaling 14 (5+9). A Queen plays next but the total remains the same (14+0).

SAMPLE GAME

1. The player to the left of the dealer begins the game. This is Player 1. One of the three

cards Player 1 has been dealt is Club 8. Player 1 picks the 8 from his hand and says "eight" while putting the card next to the draw pile.

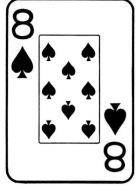

Draw Pile

2. After Player 1 plays the 8, he picks the top card from the draw pile. Each player must always have three cards in his or her hand.

3. Player 2 (to the left of Player 1) places a Jack face up on top of the 8 and gives the new score, saying "18" (8+10).

    Player 2 then picks the top card from the draw pile.

4. Player 3 (to the left of Player 2) plays a 9 face up on top of the Jack and says, "27" (18+9).

    Player 3 then picks the top card from the draw pile.

5. Player 4 (to the left of Player 3) plays a 6 face up on top of the 9 and says, "33" (27+6).

    Player 4 picks a top card from the draw pile.

6. Play continues around the table with each player playing a card and then drawing the top card from the draw pile.

7. Remember, as each card is played, the player must announce the new total score.

If you should lose track of the total you *can* go back and add the point value of the cards again.

8. Play the cards one on top of the other.

9. When you get close to 98, you should use a Queen or 10 (if you have one), in this way: The total is 92. A Queen is played, but the total is still 92 (92+0), because the Queen equals 0.

10. The next player plays a 4 on top of the Queen. The total is now 96 (92+4).

11. The next card played is a 10. The total is now 86 (96−10), because the 10 equals minus 10.

12. The idea is to try to force the other players to get 98 or more points while keeping yourself under 98.

13. The loser is the player who plays the card that causes the total to be 98 or more.

STRATEGY

1. It is good strategy to hold a Queen or a 10 until the point value of the cards already played is close to 98.

2. It is also good strategy to play high cards in the beginning of

the game and save any low
cards until the end.

HOW TO SCORE

1. The loser gets the score, which
   is 10 points for causing the total
   to be 98 or more, plus the total
   point value of the cards left in
   his or her hand.

2. When adding the score, the
   points are:

   a. Ace equals 1 point.

   b. The 2 through 9 equal their
      face value.

   c. Jack and King equal 10
      points.

3. The following is an example of
   the way Ninety-Eight is scored:
   The loser is holding a 6 and a
   4 after playing the card that
   made the total 98 or more. The
   total of these two cards is 10.
   Add 10 points for losing.

4. The score sheet looks like this:

Player 1 Player 2 Player 3 Player 4
   20   0   0   0
(10+10)

5. The game ends when one of the
   players has a total score of 100
   or more on the score sheet.

6. The winner is the player with
   the *lowest* score.

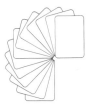

5

Fan Tan

PLAYERS

four ~~Two~~ to eight

OBJECT OF THE GAME

To be the first player out of cards

DEALER

Each player picks a card from the deck to decide who will deal. The player with the *lowest* card deals. Ace is low, King is high. The deal passes to the left with each new game.

THE DEAL

Shuffle and deal all the cards one at a time from left to right. It does not matter if some players get an extra card on the last round of the deal.

HOW TO PLAY FAN TAN

1. Each player must play a card that follows suit and sequence of number.

2. The cards rank in this order:

3. The starting card for every suit is a 7. That means until a 7 is played, no other card in that suit may be played.

4. Cards may be played next to a 7 in either direction, like this:

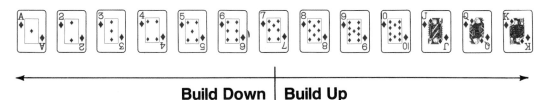

← Build Down | Build Up →

A 6 plays on one side. After the 6, you may build down to the Ace in suit and sequence of number. An 8 plays on the other side. After the 8, you may build up to the King in suit and sequence of number.

Ace is low and plays next to a 2. King is high and plays next to a Queen.

5. If a player does not have a card that will play, the player passes and does not play a card on that turn.

SAMPLE GAME

1. The player to the left of the dealer, Player 1, begins the game. Player 1 must play a 7 of any suit before any other card can be played, or else pass this turn. Player 1 plays a Club 7.

2. Player 2, to the left of Player 1,

must play a Club 6 or a Club 8 or another 7. Player 2 plays a Club 8.

3. Player 3 must play a Club 6 or a Club 9 or another 7.

   Player 3 plays a Heart 7. Notice that as a new suit—in this case Hearts—is introduced, the cards are placed in a new row. The layout looks like this.

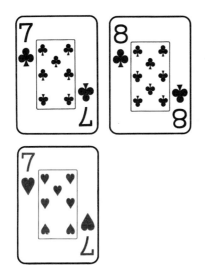

4. Player 4 can play a Club 6, a Club 9, a Heart 6, a Heart 8, or another 7. Player 4 has a Heart 6 and plays it next to the Heart 7.

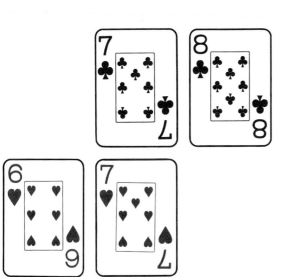

5. Play continues around the table with each player playing a card that is next in sequence and in the same suit or a 7.

6. The winner is the player who is out of cards first.

RULES TO REMEMBER

1. A player may play only one card per turn.

2. Remember, if a player cannot play a card he or she passes that turn.

STRATEGY

It is good strategy to play a card from your longest suit if you have more than one card you can play. (Your longest suit is the suit with the greatest number of cards in your hand.) For example: You are holding:

You have a choice of playing the Diamond 5 or the Heart 10.

Since Diamonds is your longest suit, you should play the Diamond 5 instead of the Heart 10.

HOW TO SCORE

1. When a player wins, all the other players count the cards left in their hand.

2. Each card is worth 1 point.

3. The winning player's score is the total number of cards left in the losing players' hands. For example:

    a. Player 1 won. Player 1 has no cards left.

    b. Player 2 has five cards left.

    c. Player 3 has nine cards left.

    d. Player 4 has three cards left.

    e. This equals 17 cards left.

4. The score sheet looks like this:

Player 1	Player 2	Player 3	Player 4
17	0	0	0

5. After each game played, the total number of points goes to the winning player.

6. Play until one player has 100 points.

6

Crazy Eights

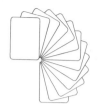

PLAYERS

Two to eight

OBJECT OF THE GAME

To be the first player out of cards

DEALER

Each player picks a card from the deck to decide who will deal. The player with the highest card is the dealer. Ace is high. The deal passes to the left with each new game.

THE DEAL

Deal the cards one at a time, beginning with the player to the left of the dealer. If there are two players, deal seven cards to each. If there are three or more players, deal five cards to each. The cards not dealt are placed in the middle of the table face down. These cards make up the draw pile. Turn up the top card of the draw pile and start a new pile of face-up cards. This new pile is the discard pile. Put the discard pile next to the draw pile.

Draw Pile

Discard Pile

If the top card turned up is an 8, bury it face down in the middle of the draw pile and turn up the next card.

HOW TO PLAY CRAZY EIGHTS

1. Sort your cards according to suits, as in this example.

2. In Crazy Eights, each player in turn plays a card from his or her hand to match the top card on the discard pile. Cards match if they are:

   a. The same suit: for example, Spade on Spade, Club on Club

   b. The same number or rank: for example, 2 on a 2, King on a King

   c. An 8 of any suit

3. The 8 of any suit is a wild card. This means that an 8 is the only card that does not have to follow suit or number. The player who plays an 8 may call any suit. For example, if a player is holding more Spades than any other suit (if Spades is the longest suit), the player may call Spades, and the next person must play a Spade or another 8.

4. Sometimes a player cannot match the top card and does not have an 8. When this

happens, the player must pick a card from the draw pile. The player must continue to pick and keep cards from the draw pile until he or she picks a card that can be played.

SAMPLE GAME

1. The person to the left of the dealer begins the game. This is Player 1. Player 1 must match the top card of the discard pile. In this sample game, Diamond 2 is the top card. Player 1 may play a Diamond, a 2 of another suit, or an 8.

    Player 1 plays a Spade 2 on the Diamond 2.

2. Player 2 must play a Spade, a 2 of another suit, or an 8.

    Player 2 plays a Spade 10. Now, Spade 10 is the top card of the discard pile.

3. Player 3 must play a Spade, a 10 of another suit, or an 8.

    Player 3 plays an 8 and calls for Hearts.

4. Player 4 may play a Heart or another 8 and call for a new suit. Player 4 does not have a Heart or an 8. Player 4 picks cards from the draw pile until he or she picks a Heart or an 8. Player 4 keeps the cards picked from the draw pile except for

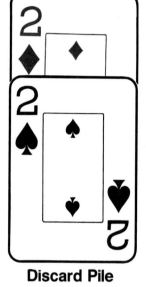

Draw Pile   **Discard Pile**

the card that can be played on the discard pile.

5. The game continues until one player gets rid of all of his or her cards. That player is the winner.

6. Sometimes it happens that no one can play a card and all the cards in the draw pile are gone. This is called a block, and the game ends. When a block occurs, the player holding the *least* number of points wins. (See scoring below.)

A RULE TO REMEMBER

A player must always play a card when it is his or her turn. A player may pass only when he or she does not have a card to play and all the cards on the draw pile are gone.

STRATEGY

Although you can use an 8 at any time, it is good strategy to save an 8 until:

a. You cannot follow suit or match the top card of the discard pile, or

b. You have several cards in one suit you want to play.

HOW TO SCORE

1. The winner of each game

receives the total amount of points left in the losers' hands.

2. This is the point value of the cards:

   a. Each 8 is worth 50 points.

   b. Each face card is worth 10 points.

   c. Each Ace is worth 1 point.

   d. All other cards equal their face value.

The players add the value of their cards. For example:

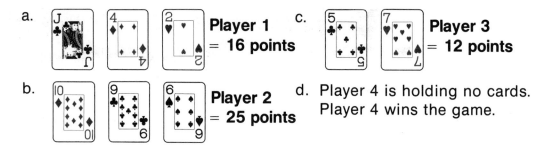

a. **Player 1** = **16 points**

b. **Player 2** = **25 points**

c. **Player 3** = **12 points**

d. Player 4 is holding no cards. Player 4 wins the game.

The score sheet looks like this:

Player 1	Player 2	Player 3	Player 4
0	0	0	53
			(16+25+12)

In case of a block, all the players add their points together. The winner is the player holding the least amount of points. The scoring is the same as in Step 3.

The first player to get 500 points wins.

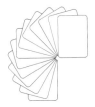

7

I Doubt It

PLAYERS

Three to six

OBJECT OF THE GAME

To be the first player out of cards

DEALER

Each player picks a card from the deck to decide who will deal. The player with the highest card is the dealer. Ace is low, King is high. The deal passes to the left with each new game.

THE DEAL

Shuffle and deal all the cards one at a time from left to right. It does not matter if some players get an extra card on the last round of the deal.

HOW TO PLAY I DOUBT IT

1. Sort your cards by number and rank, *not* by suit.

2. In this game it is fair to fool the other players by not playing the card or cards you say you are playing. However, if you are caught playing the wrong cards,

you must pay a penalty: You
must pick up all the cards on
the table.

3. Play your cards face down on
   the table so no one can see
   them.

4. Beginning with Aces, each
   player takes a turn playing from
   one to four cards face down on
   the table. After Aces are played,
   2's are played, then 3's, 4's, 5's,
   6's, 7's, 8's, 9's, 10's, Jacks,
   Queens, and Kings.

5. Actually, you may play any card
   you want but you must *pretend*
   to be playing the card it is your
   turn to play. By fooling the
   others this way, you try to be
   the first player out of cards.

6. When it is your turn, you cannot
   play more than four cards
   because there are only four
   Aces, four 2's, and so on.

   When you lay your cards down
   you must announce how many
   cards you are playing and what
   they are supposed to be—not
   what they really are. If it is your
   turn to play 9's, you say, "One
   9," or, "Two 9's," (or three 9's
   or four 9's) even if they aren't
   9's. If a player does not believe
   you, he or she says, "I doubt
   it."

1. The player to the left of the dealer (Player 1) begins the game. Player 1 must begin by playing Aces. In this sample game, Player 1 does not have an Ace, but must play a card. Player 1 decides to get rid of two cards in his hand. He plays a 7 and a Jack face down on the table and says, "Two Aces."

   No one says, "I doubt it." Everyone believes him.

2. Player 2 to the left of Player 1 continues the game. It is her turn to play 2's. Player 2 has a 2 but wants to get rid of another card, along with the 2. Player 2 plays a 2 and a 3 and says, "Two 2's." Player 1 says, "I doubt it." Player 2 has to show everyone the cards she played. Because they are not two 2's, Player 2 must pick up all the cards on the table that have been played and put them in her hand.

3. Player 3 continues the game. It is her turn to play 3's. Player 3 has one 3 and says, "One 3." No one says, "I doubt it."

4. The player to the left of Player 3 continues the game. This is Player 4, and it is his turn to play 4's. He has three 4's and he puts them face down on the table and says, "Three 4's."

Player 2 says, "I doubt it."
Player 4 shows everyone his
cards. Because the cards were
three 4's, Player 2, who doubted
him, must pick up all the cards
on the table.

5. Play continues as before with
each player taking his or her
turn playing 5's, 6's, and so on,
up to Kings. After Kings are
played, the next player begins
again with Aces.

6. The winner is the first player
out of cards.

RULES TO REMEMBER

1. Anyone may say, "I doubt it,"
but only *after* a player has
placed the cards face down on
the table, and has stated how
many and what number or rank
they are.

2. If two players say, "I doubt it"
at the same time, the player
closest to the left of the player
laying down the cards is
recognized as the "doubter."

Remember, when a player is
doubted, *all* the cards played
must be picked up by the player
or the "doubter."

STRATEGY

1. The game is more exciting and
it's easier to fool one another if
you play your cards quickly

when it is your turn.

2. It is good strategy to "doubt" a player when he or she plays the last card. It is likely the card will not be the one the player claims it is.

HOW TO SCORE

1. When a player is out of cards and wins the game, the other players count the cards left in their hand.

2. Each card is worth 1 point.

3. Each player's score is the total number of points in his or her hand. For example:

   a. Player 1 has 17 cards left.

   b. Player 2 has 15 cards left.

   c. Player 3 has 20 cards left.

   d. Player 4, the winner, has no cards.

   e. The scores are written down as follows:

Player 1	Player 2	Player 3	Player 4
17	15	20	0

4. The game ends when one of the players has a total score of 100 or more points.

5. The winner is the player with the lowest score.

8

Kings In The Corner

PLAYERS

Two to six

OBJECT OF THE GAME

To be the first player out of cards

DEALER

Each player picks a card from the deck to decide who will deal. The player with the highest card is the dealer. Ace is low, King is high. The deal passes to the left with each new game.

THE DEAL

Shuffle and deal the cards one at a time from left to right. If two people play, deal seven cards to each player. If three or more play, deal six cards to each player. After all players have been dealt their cards, deal four cards face up in the middle of the table, in the shape of a cross. Put the remaining cards, called the draw pile, face down in the middle of the cross.

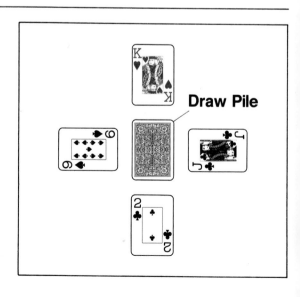

Draw Pile

HOW TO PLAY KINGS IN THE CORNER

1. In this game, each player in turn builds on the four face-up cards and also on the Kings when they are turned up.

2. To build on any of the four face-up cards, a card must be one number or rank lower and of a different color, as in this example, where the original face-up card was a Club 9.

3. A player begins by picking a card from the draw pile. After picking a card, the player begins building on the face-up cards.

4. When a King is turned up, it is put into one of the four corners until all four Kings are in a corner.

SAMPLE GAME

1. The player to the left of the dealer (Player 1) begins the game. Player 1 picks a card from the draw pile and then begins building on the cards in the middle of the table, using the cards in his hand.

   Heart King is moved to the corner. Red 10 in Player's hand plays on black Jack. Black 9 on board plays on red 10.

2. There are now two empty

spaces on the layout where the King and 9 were. Player 1 can now play two cards from his hand in the empty spaces.

3. After Player 1 completes his turn, he knocks once on the table to tell the other players he is through making plays.

4. Player 2 (to the left of Player 1) begins her turn by picking a card from the draw pile. Player 2 is holding a King in her hand. She puts the King in another corner.

   She plays a red Queen from her hand on the black King. Now the Jack, 10, and 9 can be moved to the red Queen. Player 2 now places a card from her hand in the empty space where the Jack, 10, and 9 were. She plays a black 9.

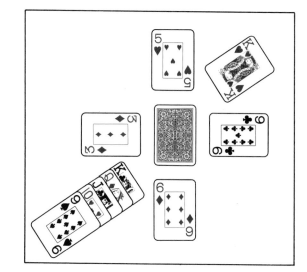

5. Player 2 knocks once when she has completed her turn.

6. Play continues around the table as above, with each player drawing a card from the draw pile before playing any cards.

7. The winner is the first player out of cards.

RULES TO REMEMBER

1. Ace is low, and no card can be played on an Ace.

2. When an empty space is created, it is filled with a card from the hand of the player who created the space.

3. Always remember to pick a card first from the draw pile when it's your turn.

4. Always remember to knock when you have completed your turn.

STRATEGY

It sometimes happens that a player does not notice a card that can be moved to another card on the layout. If this happens, no one should say anything. The next player has a chance to make that move. If the next player misses it also, then the following player has a chance.

HOW TO SCORE

1. The point value of the cards are:

   a. Kings equal 15 points.

   b. Each 10, Jack, and Queen equals 10 points.

   c. Aces equal 5 points.

   d. All other cards equal their face value.

2. All the players add the point value of their cards. For example:

a. Player 1 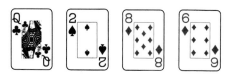 =26 points

   Player 2  =16 points

   Player 3 =10 points

   Player 4 was out of cards first = 0 points

b. Set up your score sheet like this:

Player 1	Player 2	Player 3	Player 4
26	16	10	0

c. After each game, add the points to the score under each player's name.

3. The game ends when one of the players has a total score of 100 or more.

4. The winner is the player with the lowest score.

9

Rummy

PLAYERS

Two to six

OBJECT OF THE GAME

To be the first player out of cards after obtaining or playing on sets of three of a kind, four of a kind, or a run of three or more cards

DEALER

Each player picks a card from the deck to decide who will deal. The player with the highest card is the dealer. Ace is low, King is high. After the first game the deal passes in this way:

a. If two people play, the winner of the game is the next dealer.

b. If three or more play, the deal passes to the left of the last dealer.

THE DEAL

Shuffle and deal the cards from left to right one at a time.

a. If two people play, deal ten cards to each player.

b. If three or four play, deal seven cards to each player.

c. If five or six play, deal six cards to each player.

Place the rest of the deck face down in the middle of the table. This is the draw pile. Turn up the top card and place it face up next to the draw pile. This is the discard pile.

HOW TO PLAY RUMMY

1. In this game players try to make sets or runs out of the cards in their hand, like this:

   a. A set is three or four cards of the same number or rank.

      Three Kings is a set.

      Four 9's is also a set.

   b. A run is three or more cards following suit and sequence of number.

      Spade Ace, 2, 3, is a run.

      Heart 9, 10, Jack, Queen is a run.

2. When a player has a set or run and it is his or her turn, the player lays the set or run of cards face up on the table. This is called the lay down.

3. Cards rank from Ace to King. Ace is low, King is high.

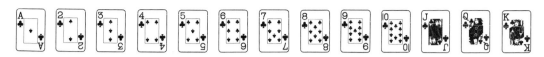

4. A player begins a turn by picking the top card from the draw pile or discard pile and ends that turn by discarding a card onto the discard pile.

5. Only the top card on the discard pile may be picked up. All the cards under the top card are dead cards. They are buried and cannot be used.

6. Sort the cards in your hand according to runs or sets.

---

1. Player 1 to the left of the dealer begins the game by picking the top card from the draw pile or discard pile.

Player 1

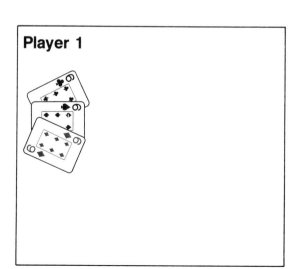

a. Player 1 picks a Club 6 from the draw pile. Player 1 is holding a Spade 6, Diamond 6, Club 2, Club 9, Diamond 10, Diamond Queen, and Spade King.

b. With the Club 6, Player 1 has a set of three 6's. Player 1's lay down looks like this.

c. Player 1 discards the Spade King face up on the discard pile. Player 1's turn ends.

2. Player 2 begins by picking the top card from the draw pile or the discard pile.

   a. Player 2 picks the Spade King from the discard pile. Player 2 holds Diamond Ace, Diamond 3, Heart 6, Spade Jack, Diamond Jack, Diamond King, and Club King.

   b. With the Spade King, Player 2 now has a set of three Kings. Player 2 also has a Heart 6 that matches Player 1's set of 6's. Player 2 puts the Heart 6 next to Player 1's set of 6's, and lays down the set of Kings. Player 2's lay down looks like this:

   c. Player 2 discards the Diamond Jack.

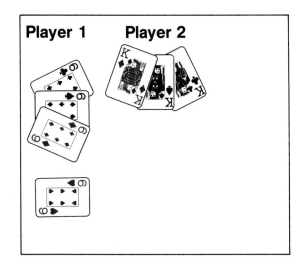

3. Player 3 begins his or her turn.

   a. Player 3 picks a Spade 8 from the draw pile. Player 3 holds Spade Ace, Heart Ace, Spade 9, Spade 10, Heart 10, Club Queen, and Spade Queen.

   b. With the Spade 8, Player 3 has a Spade run. Player 3's lay down looks like this:

   c. Player 3 discards the Heart 10, ending the turn.

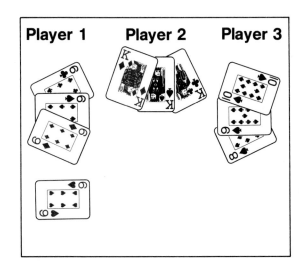

Play continues around the
table until one player lays down
all his or her cards and wins the
game.

RULES TO REMEMBER

1. Only when it is a player's turn
   may he or she lay down a set or
   a run or a card that fits with
   another player's set or run.

2. A player begins his or her turn
   by drawing the top card from
   the draw pile or discard pile.
   That turn ends by discarding a
   card onto the discard pile.

3. The top card on the discard pile
   must cover all the other cards
   on the discard pile. It is not fair
   to look at the cards that have
   already been discarded.

STRATEGY

1. It is important that players
   watch the other players'
   discards.

   a. By watching discards, a
      player knows when a card
      needed to complete a set or
      run has been discarded and
      is buried in the discard pile.
      A player can then rearrange
      his or her hand and try for
      another set or run.

   b. By watching discards, a
      player also learns what the
      other players are saving and

may prevent them from winning by not discarding cards the other players need to complete a set or run.

2. When discarding, always get rid of a high unmatched card in your hand. This will help your score if you lose, because high cards count against you.

HOW TO SCORE

1. The winner of each game receives the total amount of points left in the losers' hands.

2. The point value of the cards are:

   a. Ace equals 1 point.

   b. King, Queen, Jack equal 10 points.

   c. All other cards equal their face value.

3. The losing players total their points, like this:

   a. Player 1 = 30 points   b. Player 2 = 17 points

   c. Player 3 has no cards. Player 3 wins the game.

4. The score sheet looks like this:

Player 1	Player 2	Player 3
0	0	47(30+17)

5. The winner is the player who gets 200 points first.

48